Understanding Business Financing and Investments

Geary Reid

ISBN: 978-976-8305-96-1

Acknowledgments

Great thanks must be expressed to the following people:

The heavenly Father, for granting me the wisdom and inspiration to record the information in this book, which I began on May 18, 2022, and completed on May 23, 2022; my family, for their continued encouragement and support regarding various challenges; and several people who have assisted with reviewing and editing the book:

- Satesh Naraine, ACCA
- Shellon Garner, ACCA, CAT
- Lance France Cummings, MSc., FCCA
- Dane Gibson, ACCA
- Dexter Cox, MBA

To you, the reader: have fun while reading, and grasp and practice what you learn so that this world will become a better place. Many people are depending on your guidance. We all need a shoulder to lean on and a hand to guide us.

Geary Reid

MBA, FCCA, FAAPM, MPM, CA

Reid's Learning Institute and Business Consultancy

reidnlearn.com

Amazon: amazon.com/author/gearyreid

Facebook: Reid n Learn

Instagram: Reid n Learn

LinkedIn: Reid's Learning Institute
and Business Consultancy

199 Kuru - Kururu, Soesdyke Linden Highway
Guyana, South America

Table of Contents

Introduction

Securing financing is a challenging task for many business owners. Some businesses remain small or even fail because the owners were unable to access additional funds to grow their businesses.

Why businesses borrow money is an important question that many people ask and need to know the answer. There are several reasons why businesses borrow money, and one primary reason is to offset liabilities. It is a difficult situation when business owners borrow money to settle liabilities, though, because they have to repay both sets of liabilities.

Business owners who desire to borrow money for their business need to know that there are criteria that must be met before they can borrow. If the criteria are not met, then the potential borrower will not be able to access the funds needed. Business owners must ensure that their financial statements are current and, if applicable, audited in order to easily meet the requirements of lending institutions.

Business owners must choose if they need short- or long-term loans. The requirements for short- and long-term loans have many commonalities, but there are some differences between these two types of loans. In addition, debt financing and equity financing are different. However, business owners can decide if they want to increase their debt or if they are willing to share part of the ownership of the business with others. The financial structure of the business must be assessed regularly once the business increases its liabilities. Once the funds borrowed accrue interest, then the managers must properly account for the borrowing costs according to the appropriate International Financial Reporting Standards.

Before a business chooses to engage in investment, the owners and managers must record all the appropriate costs. Initially, the managers will have to estimate costs, and then those costs, once carefully assessed, must be included in the budget. Once the actual cost is incurred, then it must be evaluated against budget. Each investment must also have a timeline established. Each capital investment must allow the business owners to increase revenue, reduce cost, or provide some economic benefits to the business. Before embarking on any capital investment, the business owner must have confidence that the project will generate a net cash inflow to the business.

The bank and cash balances must be carefully managed. Parts of funds owned by the business can be invested once there is no urgent need for such funds. Financial ratios are often used to evaluate the financial performance of the business. However, financial ratios have limitations.

Some business owners need to borrow money to expand their businesses. They must carefully use the funds borrowed for their intended purpose. Over the years, the business must grow and attract more customers, more revenue, and more net cash flow.

Section 1: Borrowing

In this section, many aspects of borrowing are carefully addressed. Many questions about borrowing also are asked and answered.

Both academic and practical information are provided concerning borrowing. Once business owners use the information and suggestions provided in this literature, then they can access the money their business needs. Many business owners do not know some of the requirements they must have when they are seeking financing.

Long-term and short-term borrowing must be considered by business owners. Both have different requirements, but there are many aspects that are common to both types of borrowing.

1. Why do businesses borrow money?

Managing a business is far different than managing a household since household income and expenses (grocery, rent, utility bills and the like) are usually stable and predictable. On the other hand, a business often encounters unstable income and fixed expenses that must be covered, regardless of income. Simply put, one member of the family can manage the entire family's finances, yet a business would require several academic and experienced persons to manage such finances.

Not all businesses will have the funds they need. Due to the lack of adequate funds, there may be a strong reason to seek additional financing. Business owners and managers may be against seeking financing, given the cost or interest payments associated with borrowing, but sometimes, the plans and projects they intend to execute demand large sums of money.

1.1 Startups

Startup businesses are similar to babies that are heavily dependent on their parents for support. Many startup businesses still need their owners to inject more and more funds into them before any significant return is realized.

Beyond the great ideas many business owners have, they need enough money to translate their business ideas into profitable ventures. If the owners do not have the funds needed, then they will have to borrow the funds for their startup businesses.

There is no established point in time when startup businesses will become totally independent of their owners' injections of money. Most owners want their startup businesses to become financially independent within a few days, but those few days may turn into months and years. Therefore, the owner must adequately finance the business and regularly monitor its performance so that the business will become profitable and start generating enough funds to settle expenses as well as have some remaining for reinvestments.

Many startup business owners share the same challenge of lacking adequate financing and thus the need to raise money. In some countries, there are financial institutions that are set up to assist businesses like these with microfinances, financing, or joint ventures.

Before startup, business owners can approach a financial institution for financing, but they may be required to produce a business plan. The business plan will include information on the intended direction of the business, amount of funds needed, marketing plans, and mission statements, among others. The business plan must include the information that the business owners have in their heads that then is translated into a written document. Many business owners have great ideas in their heads, but they must learn to put their ideas into writing. The business plan must be simple enough for the financial institution to understand and thereby influence their decision to assist the business with financing.

1.2 Restocking

Some businesses will need additional finances for the purpose of restocking. The business owners may choose to replenish their stocks, especially if they allow credit sales and are awaiting those customers to settle their balances.

Some owners may choose to increase their stocks to cater to future sales. During winter and summer seasons, some owners may choose to increase their inventories because of anticipated seasonal demand from customers. There are some products that are seasonal, so business owners must ensure that they have enough inventories to match the needs of their customers during those seasons. Previous sales history and industry statistics can be good guides to inform business owners how much capital they will need to increase their inventories for future periods.

Business owners may seek financing to increase their inventories because they will enjoy discounts for large-volume purchases. Some suppliers will only offer discounts to customers once they purchase a specific volume. Sometimes, the discount obtained can be a major financial relief to business owners because the lower unit selling price will make the business competitive.

1.3 Acquiring land and buildings

Both startup and mature businesses will have opportunities to acquire land and buildings. The locations where some land and buildings are available for sale are prime locations. Those locations positively impact goodwill and allow businesses to leapfrog their competition and become great businesses. Sometimes, key location is all that is needed for the success of a business.

When land and buildings are available for sale, business owners may not have all the funds needed to acquire them; therefore, they will have to seek financing. If business owners do not purchase the land and buildings on time, then other business owners may purchase them. When opportunities are lost, they may never return, so it is important to be alert and agile enough to capture significant opportunities.

In some countries, land is difficult to acquire. Most times, there are small portions of land available and many potential buyers. Therefore, those who are interested in that land and those buildings must have access to finances almost immediately.

When a business acquires a portion of land, there will be the need for further development. However, the first thing that must be done is to acquire the land, and then development will follow.

1.4 Expansion opportunities

Business owners must look for expansion opportunities. There are often many opportunities that will cause some businesses to grow, and business owners must be vigilant to maximize those opportunities. Too many owners are myopic; that is to say, they are narrow minded in their business visions. They become complacent or comfortable about their businesses and the locations they occupy. Some businesses are in existence for many decades and never grow because the owners lack the vision to expand the businesses. Figure 1 lists several of the main reasons businesses will expand.

Figure 1. Strategic reasons for expanding businesses

(All figures developed by the author unless otherwise noted.)

1.4.1 Change of Head Office

Some business owners will change their head office location. They may decide on another location that allows them to be closer to their value chain, including their customers, suppliers, and distributors, in addition to being closer to the capital city. Whatever reason they have for changing their locations, though, must be a strategic reason. Often, reconstructing the head office is a costly project. Therefore, some business owners will seek financing for such a project. Most times, with new head offices, the owners will include some of the amenities they did not have in the previous locations. Very rarely will business owners construct small head offices.

1.4.2 More stores

Owners may also want to sell more products to the market. They will recognize the need to establish more brick-and-mortar stores to reach more customers. Many customers want easy access to stores, especially if they need to physically see and touch the products they intend to purchase.

Business owners may raise additional financing to open new stores that will allow them to have adequate products for customers' immediate purchase. Business owners need to ensure that those stores are appealing to customers in order to provide an ideal shopping environment.

1.4.3 Parking lots

With parking lots, many customers will feel comfortable shopping at businesses. The absence of parking lots has caused some customers to only shop at places where they are able to safely park their vehicles.

Business owners who need to attract more customers will have to consider making adequate parking available. Even if the business owners do not have the money to develop the parking lots, they can seek financing to have that important facility available for customers' benefit. In some communities, business owners will purchase land and buildings from persons who are neighbors to the business because that land can be used for parking lots. Even though the business owners might not need the buildings situated on that land, they will have to purchase both land and buildings just to benefit from use of the land.

Some of the land where persons have their homes may be extremely costly. However, if the business owners need that land to convert into parking lots, then they will have to negotiate with the owners for a reasonable selling price. Once they both agree on the selling price, then the business owners will have to acquire the financing and make their payments.

1.4.4 Building warehouses

Warehouses are key to many businesses since they must have adequate space to hold inventories. Even small businesses need somewhere to store inventory.

At the start of some businesses, they have small warehouses; however, as the businesses expand, the owners will have need for more warehouse space. If business owners want to benefit from volume discounts when purchasing inventories, then they will be required to purchase larger volumes.

Most times, the construction of new and larger warehouses will be expensive. Some business owners will prefer to borrow money to construct such warehouses. New warehouses must be built with many modern facilities, such as fire alarms and security systems. Usually, when a warehouse is being built, the owners build with a plan for the warehouse to be usable long into the future.

Expansion of existing warehouses may also be a costly project that may result in the business owners' seeking financing. Expanding warehouses may be necessary to meet the increasing demands from customers. Once customers increase their shopping, then it is important for business owners to have the products that customers need. Regular inventory outages will result in some customers shopping with competitors where all of their needs are readily met.

1.4.5 Economies of scale

Owners also may expand their businesses to benefit from economies of scale. For example, with larger warehouses, businesses will purchase more inventories at lower unit costs. When businesses expand, some costs will not increase since those costs are fixed. For instance, even when businesses have more stores, they may not have to increase their promotion costs, especially if they are engaged in radio and television advertising.

The average cost of production may decline when the business expands since the employees will not have to perform additional duties, even though they are producing more. The logistical costs when acquiring inventory may remain the same as well when businesses expand. Therefore, some business owners will seek financing to expand their businesses because they will benefit from lower unit costs and selling prices to customers.

1.4.6 New markets

New markets provide many opportunities for businesses to increase revenue, and this may lead business owners to set up new stores. New markets also may encourage business owners to increase their production. The new market will also cause businesses to acquire more inventories. Thus, entering new markets may result in the need for additional financing.

1.4.7 New products

New products often require more money to produce. Sometimes, to produce new products, business owners will have to acquire new machines, new equipment, new software, and additional warehouse space. Although owners want to produce new products, they may need additional financing for day-to-day operations due to exhaustion of their current business finances.

If business owners want to increase their efficiency, they may have to change their operations and machinery. Some modern machines and equipment are expensive, and business owners may not have enough funds to purchase them; hence, they will have to borrow money to make the purchases.

1.4.8 Increase in profit

Many times, business owners will expand their businesses to increase their profits. When businesses are not making much profit, their owners tend to worry. However, in order for some businesses to experience increases in profits, they may have to expand their operations. As they seek to increase their profits, they may have to finance these expansions of the businesses.

1.4.9 Spreading risks

Owners sometimes seek to expand their businesses because they want to spread their risks. For example, the owners may be operating their business in one country but may choose to expand into other countries. Business owners who are producing one product may choose to add more products to meet the needs of other customers. Businesses that have small warehouses may need to increase their warehouse space to meet the needs of most customers.

Spreading risks may result in the business's having to expand some of its operations. The expansion of the business will require finances, which may have to be borrowed because the business owners have exhausted their funds.

1.5 Investments

Whenever there is need for extensive investments, many owners will prepare their business plans and submit those plans to financial institutions. Investments can be large sums of money, and major investments will take much time to complete.

Business owners will generally prefer to borrow money for their investments. They will keep their finances for their daily operations while the borrowed money will be used for investments.

1.6 Changing the fleet of vehicles

To be competitive, many businesses that sell products must have enough vehicles to transport their products to their stores, warehouses, and customers. Newer vehicles have many new features that often make customers feel valued. Figure 2 lays out the numerous reasons businesses refresh their vehicle fleets.

Figure 2. Reasons why businesses change their fleets of vehicles

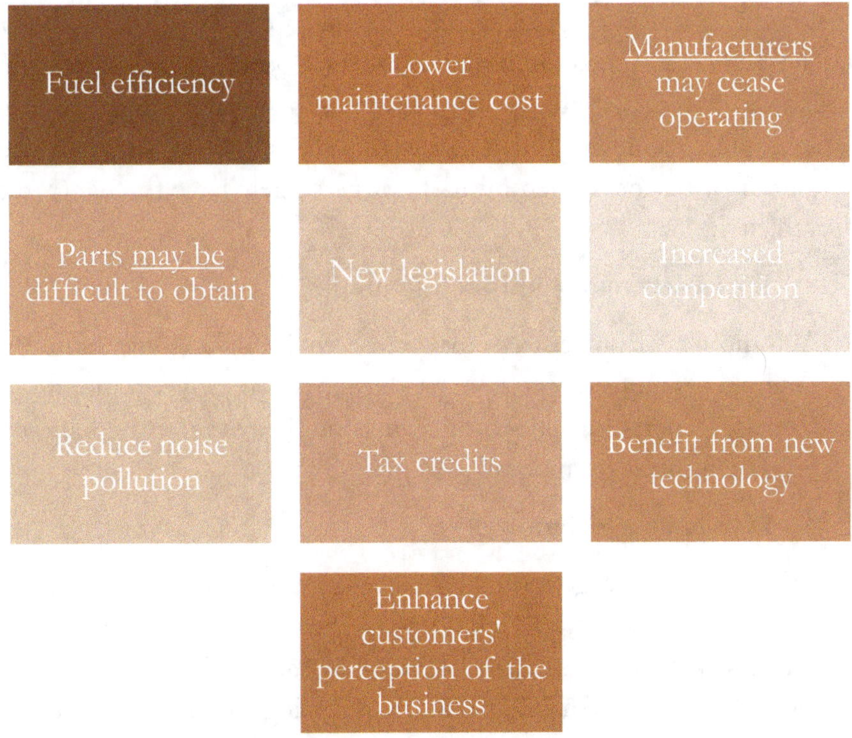

1.6.1 Fuel efficiency

Most business owners are always concerned about the costs of fuel. When fuel costs increase, business will experience increases in operational costs, which may result in lower profits.

New fleets of vehicles are often more fuel efficient. Those new vehicles will travel the same distance but use less fuel. Because the new vehicles use less fuel, there is less cost to the business.

1.6.2 Lower maintenance cost

Old vehicles often have higher maintenance costs even if the owners constantly maintain those vehicles. Old vehicles will sometimes suddenly stop working despite recently repairs. Therefore, if business owners need to lower their vehicle-maintenance costs, then acquiring a new fleet of vehicles will be their answer.

1.6.3 Manufacturers may cease operating

Replacing a fleet of vehicles may not be an owner's first choice, but the vehicle manufacturer may cease to operate. Some automobile manufacturers cease to operate because of high labor costs, high costs to acquire materials, or increases in competition. When manufacturers go out of business, then business owners likely have to change their vehicle fleets.

1.6.4 Parts maybe difficult to obtain

Automobile manufacturers may cease to produce some parts. For example, manufacturers will produce new models or modify the models, so parts for older models may not be manufactured and may soon be difficult or impossible to find.

1.6.5 New legislation

From time to time, governments will change legislation. Some of these changes may impact the choice of vehicles in the country. Those vehicles that produce large quantities of carbon dioxide may attract higher taxes or even be banned from being imported. Remember, government has a responsibility to protect the economy and the environment and not just to protect any specific business.

Greenhouse emission has been a major topic of discussion since many countries are affected both positively and negatively by changes in weather that are impacted by air pollution due to carbon dioxide from vehicles and processing plants. Some business owners may change their fleets of vehicles because new legislation may prevent the use of vehicles that contribute to noise pollution.

1.6.6 Increased competition

When there are other businesses within the same sector, then there will be constant competition. Businesses may change their fleets of vehicles because their competitors have changed theirs. Competitors are often looking for ways to increase their sales and profits, so companies must look at and learn from their competitors.

1.6.7 Reduce noise pollution

Some older vehicles contribute significantly to noise pollution. Therefore, some owners may change those older vehicles because of the noise that are made by those vehicles.

1.6.8 Tax credits

Governments may offer tax credits to buyers of new vehicles. With tax credits, businesses that acquire new vehicles will pay lower taxes or may be able to reclaim taxes paid to acquire the vehicles. Businesses that are involved in tax planning often look for opportunities to pay lower taxes, so acquiring new fleets of vehicles may allow some businesses to claim tax credits.

1.6.9 Benefit from new technology

New vehicles often come with new technology. Therefore, purchasers of new vehicles will benefit from that technology.

Years ago, drivers had to remember where some places were located or use a physical map if they had to visit customers. However, many new vehicles have global positioning systems (GPSs), so if a driver wants to go to a new place for the first time, they can do so by inserting the address of the place, and they will be guided by the GPS.

Lorry drivers who must deliver cargo to new locations do not have to depend upon detailed guidance from the customers but can simply enter the customers' addresses into the GPS and then be guided to the customers.

1.6.10 Enhance customers' perception of the business

Customers sometimes shop at some businesses because they perceive that the businesses are a good reflection of themselves. Customers want to know that the money they spend at a business is used to increase the value of the business. New fleets of vehicles make some customers feel connected to the business, and customers' perception is critical for the survival of most businesses.

1.7 Repaying suppliers

Business owners may seek short-term financing because they must settle their outstanding balances with their suppliers. Some suppliers will offer short-term credit, usually for 30 days, but once that time is up, then the customer must settle the outstanding balances.

Although business owners project to have cash inflow to offset their liabilities, their projections may not always be correct. One such liability that must be settled in a timely manner is the repayment of suppliers' balances.

2. Factors affecting how much money businesses can borrow

Although business owners may know that they need financing, they may be uncertain of the amount to borrow.

Borrowers . . . need money to finance their purchases. This includes businesses that need money to finance their investments or to expand their inventories as well as individuals who borrow money to purchase a new car or a new home. (Titman et al., 2016, p. 20)

2.1 Factors impacting borrowers' ability to obtain financing

There are many factors that will impact a business's ability to obtain financing as shown in Figure 3. These factors can be numerous for some businesses and may result in some business owners no longer being interested in raising money. Sometimes, business owners and individuals feel that they must provide too much detail just to get funding. Although the business owners may provide the documents needed, their loan application may be turned down, or they may receive a lesser amount than they requested.

Figure 3. Factors impacting how much money businesses can borrow

2.1.1 Audited financial statements

Businesses that are incorporated under the relevant laws of their home countries will be required to prepare and file annual audited financial statements at a designated agency. When financial institutions are considering lending money to businesses, they may request copies of these audited financial statements for current previous years in order to assess the financial viability of the business. The audited financial statements must be approved by members of the board or non-executive directors for larger businesses (publicly traded).

The audited financial statements contain some key statements and notes. Generally, the notes on the accounts can be numerous and will vary from business to business, but there is some basic financial information that must be contained in the audited financial statements, as shown in Figure 4.

Figure 4. Basic financial statements

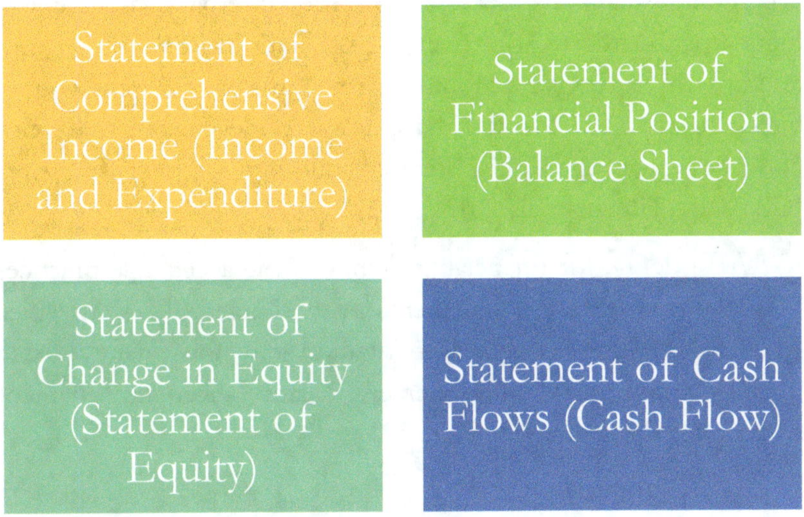

(Extracted from Titman et al., 2016)

The audited financial statements contain much important information about the business's past performance. Each year's financial statements will cover 12 months of financial performance. The 12 months can be 12 calendar months starting from January or 12 months from the business's anniversary date.

The financial institution will evaluate the business's audited financial statements to assess its past performance. If the financial institution needs more details to support the figures in the audited financial statements, then they can request that information to determine the business's ability to obtain financing.

The notes on the financial statements are often limited in terms of details. Those notes are often prepared according to the accounting standards that the business follows. Most businesses will use the International Financial Reporting Standards (IFRS), International Accounting Standards (IAS), or the generally accepted accounting principles (GAAP) to guide the preparation and presentation of their audited financial statements.

International Financial Reporting Standards (IFRS) are a set of accounting standards set out by the International Accounting Standards Board (IASB). The [IASBs] and [IFRSs] arose from an attempt to harmonise accounting standards in different countries, which began in 1973. [IFRSs] have now been adopted by all developed countries except the United States . . . and Japan, which use their own [GAAPs]. (Titman et al., 2016, p. 45)

[GAAPs] define for financial accountants the acceptable practices in preparation of financial statements in the United States. Specifically, [GAAPs] tell [the] financial accountant exactly how financial data has to show up on the income statement, balance sheet and statement of cash flows. (Loughram, 2011, p. 52)

2.1.2 Collateral

Financial institutions will request collateral whenever an individual or business approaches them for financing. That collateral is often needed to determine ownership of certain assets by the individual or business. If the business recently started and does not have ownership over some assets, then that may be an impediment to the business's being able to obtain financing from the financial institution. Examples of such collateral are shown in Figure 5.

Figure 5. Collateral required by lending institutions

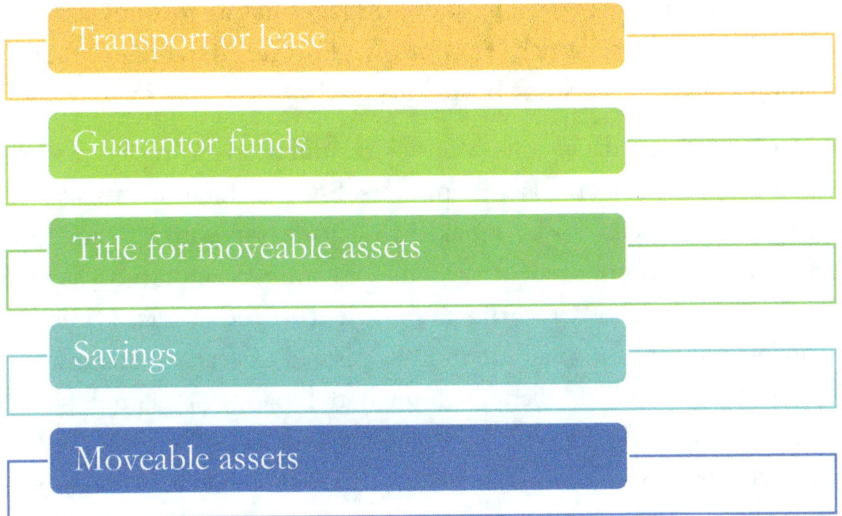

Many small and startup businesses do not possess any savings, so whatever money the business owners have, they will reinvest back into the business. Therefore, if the financial institution requests to see substantial amounts in their savings accounts, then that will not be possible for many businesses.

Some businesses will have moveable assets. However, businesses that recently started may rent properties until they can acquire their own. Such business owners may not have leases and transports since they do not have ownership of the land.

2.1.3 Cost of investment

The cost of investment will reflect the amount of money needed for the project or activities. For example, the cost of investment to construct a building will be the full cost from start to finish. The financial institution may not provide the full cost of the investment, but they need to know how much the project will cost. The cost of investment to acquire a vehicle will be the full cost that has to be paid to the supplier to acquire the vehicle.

2.1.4 Duration

The duration to repay loans and mortgages has a great impact on the decision of how much to borrow. Shorter durations often put additional strain on some borrowers.

Many financial institutions offer longer durations to repay mortgages and loans for specific, larger amounts. Shorter durations will result in larger installments to be repaid in a shorter amount of time. Some financial institutions will offer loans for a longer duration because they earn more interest from the amount lent to the clients. Oftentimes, financial institutions will use months instead of years to determine the duration over which clients will repay the loan. For example, instead of referring to the loan being offered as one for 2 years, the client will be told that they have 24 months to repay the loan. If the loan is provided for 5 years, then the client will be told that they have 60 months to repay the loan.

2.1.5 Interest rate

Many times, business owners want to borrow money from financial institutions, but when they know the interest rate, they may borrow less or may not borrow at all. The interest rate will impact the installment and total amount repaid.

Table 1. Different interest rates for $300,000 to be borrowed by PJA

Description	Scenario 1	Scenario 2	Scenario 3	Scenario 4
Amount to be borrowed	$300,000	$300,000	$300,000	$300,000
Interest rate	10%	20%	30%	40%

Repayment duration (months)	12	12	12	12
Interest + principal	$330,000	$360,000	$390,000	$420,000
Installments (per month)	$27,500	$30,000	$32,500	$35,000

Table 1 provides an illustration of $300,000 to be borrowed by PJA. The duration to repay the loan is fixed at 12 months. However, PJA has four scenarios from four financial institutions from which to choose. If PJA chooses Scenario 1, then the monthly installment for 12 months will be $27,500. If PJA choose Scenario 4, then the monthly installment for 12 months will be $35,000. The four scenarios will also impact the collateral the borrowers need to submit. If borrowers are highly indebted, then they may have to pay a higher interest rate for the loan to compensate the lender for the increased risk.

2.1.6 Income

Business owners who want to borrow need to prove that they are generating revenue. Their monthly or annual earnings will determine how much they can borrow.

Lower earnings will result in smaller amounts being lent. Although two businesses may have the same store sizes, if their earnings are different, they will likely be eligible to borrow different amounts or eligible for different repayment durations, all because of their earnings.

Some financial institutions will establish the portion of the earnings that will be used to service amounts borrowed. For example, some financial institutions may establish that 25%, 30%, 35%, or 40% of the business's income will be used to service the loan. So, even though business owners may want to borrow larger amounts, they will not be eligible for amounts that are beyond the portion of their earnings that will be used to repay the loan.

2.1.7 Debt ratio

Before financial institutions offer loans to businesses, they will have to evaluate how much debt the borrowers have. Those businesses who have borrowed large amounts but have small asset values will find it difficult to obtain large loans.

It is common practice to describe a firm's financial structure using the debt ratio, which is the proportion of a firm's assets that have been financed by liabilities. (Titman et al., 2016, p. 484)

2.1.8 Borrower's contribution

When seeking financing, borrowers often must make their own contributions. They are expected to show evidence that they will provide part of the cost of the investment. For example, if the financial institution agreed to contribute towards the financing of an investment of $500,000, they may require the borrower to provide a down payment or deposit of 10%. Therefore, the borrower's contribution will be $50,000. If the borrower is unable to obtain financing from another institution but is required to make a contribution of 20% for the same investment cost of $500,000, then the borrower must make a deposit of $100,000 as their contribution towards the cost of the investment.

2.1.9 Risk preference

If the business is a partnership or has many directors, then some of those owners may have their own risk preferences. Although many of the owners and managers know what must be done, they may not want to borrow large sums of money because they feel that they will not be able to repay the full amount borrowed. There are three main types of risk preference, which are presented in Table 2.

Table 2. Risk preferences

Risk Preference	Explanation
Risk averse	A decision maker who acts on the assumption that the worst outcome might occur
Risk neutral	A decision maker who is concerned with what will be the most likely outcome
Risk seeker	A decision maker who is interested in the best outcome no matter how small the chance that it may occur

(Extracted from BPP Learning Media, 2010)

2.1.10 Operating expenses

Although businesses may have large incomes, their expenses may also be high. High expenses reduce the amount of money the business will have available to service the loans. Most business owners who want large loans must prove that their net operating profit will be significant enough to service the loan. Their net operating profit will be the results of them deducting all their expenses against the revenue they earned.

Financial institutions will also ask business owners to provide a copy of their current year's budget. This budget, along with copies of the audited financial statements, will provide evidence of the business's ability to repay the amount borrowed.

2.1.11 Liquidity position

Even if businesses are profitable, they may have liquidity problems. Most of their cash inflows will be used to repay high-liability balances. Most businesses that are seeking financing will be delighted if their liability balance is small and if they have healthy cash balances.

Liquidity is the amount of cash a company can obtain quickly to settle its debts (and possibly to meet other unforeseen demands for cash payments too). (BPP Learning Media, 2010)

A liquid business is highly likely to have money to repay its installments.

2.1.12

Most financial institutions have software to assess the credit scores of borrowers. The financial institution will request specific information from the borrower, and after that information is received, it will be processed in the software, and a financial result will be produced. Based upon the score from the software, the financial institution will determine the amount and duration and interest rate of the loan to be offered. Businesses that have previous borrowing history with financial institutions and were able to repay their installments on or before the due date may be eligible to borrow once again. Good credit history will give some borrowers an advantage versus those businesses who have poor credit histories with those or other financial institutions.

3. Sources of money

When individuals and businesses need financing, there are several sources from which they can borrow. However, the various financiers have their own advantages and disadvantages. Borrowers must carefully evaluate each source before deciding from whom and when to borrow.

3.1 Families

When business owners need financing, they may discuss the matter with their families. They will often approach family members who possess wealth to assist them with the needed financing. There are some family members who are willing to support other relatives who have businesses and need financial assistance.

Family financing can be easy to obtain since the borrower likely does not have to pledge any security in exchange for the funds to be borrowed. The arrangement between the borrower and lender may be based on verbal communication since neither person may sign any legal document.

One drawback with seeking financing from family is that they may not be able to provide financing for longer periods. Therefore, the repayment period may be very short. Another drawback is that if the lender becomes upset with the borrower, the borrower may be asked to repay the funds immediately, which will be an embarrassing situation and potentially difficult to find the funds for repayment on short notice.

3.2 Friends

Another good source to access financing is through friends. Some persons have many friends who are wealthy, and some of those friends are willing to provide financial assistance. There are friends who want to help a friend's business become successful, so they will do what they can to help.

With funds provided through friends, there may not be any legal agreements to sign. Also, no security may have to be offered when borrowing from friends. Also, the funds from friends may be interest free and may have no late fees if the full amount is not paid on time.

However, drawbacks from borrowing from friends include the fact that the amounts to be provided may be small and the repayment periods may be short. If the friendship is fragile, then the amount borrowed may have to be repaid almost immediately if there is a falling out.

3.3 Credit unions

Individuals who have business may have savings with credit unions. Their savings with the credit unions might have started before the establishment of their business.

Individuals who are saving with credit unions will find it easy to borrow whenever they have needs and meet the union's requirements. The interest rates at most credit unions are relatively low compared to those at many banks. Members who want to borrow from credit unions may not have to provide many documents since the credit union already has information about them. The borrower is often required to have the backing of a guarantor for the funds they need to borrow. Since members can borrow from the credit union relatively easily, the loan may be approved very quickly.

The limitation with credit union borrowing is that the amount to be borrowed may be based on the amount that the member has saved with the credit union. There are some credit unions that will lend members two to three times the amounts they have saved. For example, if a member has $100,000 and is entitled to three times that amount, then the member will only be entitled to borrow $300,000. Another limitation with credit union borrowing is that the amount that some members may need in a time of emergency may be above the amount that the credit union can lend. So, if a member needs $500,000, $300,000 will not meet their needs, and they will have to seek additional financing.

Credit unions have to protect their money, so they will only lend to their members. Sometimes, members will have to complete several years of saving with the credit union before they are entitled to large borrowing.

3.4 Financial Institutions

Many financial institutions have funds to lend to potential borrowers. However, the borrowers will have to provide some important documents and prove their ability to repay the funds.

Business owners will approach financial institutions to borrow because they may be eligible for larger amounts than they would be from the aforementioned sources. They may also approach financial institutions because they need longer durations to repay the amounts they need.

A detriment to borrowing from financial institution is the interest rates they will charge. Another potentially negative aspect of using financial institutions is that they will often require many details and personal documents before they offer financial assistance.

4. Debt financing

Business owners may seek debt financing because they do not want to transfer part of the ownership of the business to anyone else. Those owners will take on the full risk of the business and will use whatever finances they receive to manage the business and to repay the money borrowed.

4.1 Secured debt financing

For debt financing, business owners may seek secured financing whereby they have to provide some form of security in order to borrow funds. Many times, financial institutions will need some assets or something of value they can sell in the event the borrowers fail to honor their obligation. Financial institutions may accept transport of lands, vehicle registrations, or guarantors before providing secured financing.

However, a benefit of secured debt financing often is lower interest rates on the loans. The financial institution will provide a lower or more affordable interest rate because they have something that was used to secure the loan in the event the borrower defaults.

4.2 Unsecured debt financing

Unlike secured debt financing, unsecured debt financing is not backed by any security for the loan. In some cases, financial institutions will take the risk of providing unsecured loans. The financial institution may choose to provide unsecured loans to repeat borrowers or even to borrowers who need small-value loans. The interest rate on unsecured loans is often higher than the interest rate on secured loans since they are inherently riskier for the lender.

Usually, unsecured loans are given only to credit-worthy borrowers. The borrowers will have to provide much information about their sources of income, which will indicate their ability to repay their loans.

"Longer-term unsecured issues are usually called debentures; shorter-term issues are usually termed notes" (Bradley & Myers, 1991, p. 597).

4.3 Revolving debt and credit cards

Some borrowers can approach the same financial institutions from which they have borrowed and access loans on a regular basis. They may be able to secure additional loans frequently because they have a revolving loan agreement with the financial institution. For example, a credit card is a revolving loan. With the credit card, once the customers settle their balances, then they can continue with future spending up to their credit limits and repeat that process as often as they like.

4.4 Lines of credit

Some financial institutions will offer lines of credit (LOCs) to customers. A line of credit allows the borrower to write checks or withdraw funds whenever they are ready. Line of credit is often provided to customers based on how credit worthy they are. Business owners may utilize lines of credit to replenish their inventory for upcoming seasons when they anticipate customers will need certain products.

The line of credit provided to customers will vary, but there will be a maximum amount the customer can borrow. Some financial institutions will offer lines of credit to customers who are with them for many years. Sometimes, banks will offer lines of credit to their customers for the Christmas season, which will allow the customer to have additional spending power for that specific period.

4.5 Bank overdrafts

Business owners can secure overdrafts from financial institutions because of their previous financial histories. The interest rate on overdrafts is higher because they are loans given on demand.

Overdrafts are often provided to fill the gap of brief shortages for businesses. Overdrafts usually have additional fees, though.

4.6 Bonds issued

Borrowers may request financing for their business through the use of bonds. The borrowers will determine the amount of funds they need and then arrange to issue bonds. When borrowers issue bonds, they are seeking financing from the public, and in return, they will provide the public a fixed interest rate and thus fixed payments for providing their financing to help the business. Before a business can issue bonds, it must receive approval from the government, financial institution, or regulatory authority in its country. Governments often issue treasury bills and bonds to secure funds for future projects. Table 3 provides some basic terminology for bonds.

Bonds that are issued by corporations are often referred to as corporate bonds. Thus, a corporate bond is a security sold by a corporation, which has future payments and a maturity date. (Titman et al., 2016, p. 259)

Table 3. Bond terminology

Terms	Explanation
Indenture	The legal agreement between a firm issuing the bonds and the bond trustee who represents the bondholders. It lists the specific terms of the loan agreement, including a description of the bonds, the rights of the bondholders, the rights of the issuing firm, and the responsibilities of the trustee.
Priority of claim on assets and income	In the case of insolvency, claims of debt in general, including bonds, are honored before those of both ordinary and preference (sometimes known as preferred) shares. In

	addition, interest payments hold priority over dividend payments for ordinary and preference shares.
Face value	The face value of a bond, also known as its par value, is the principal that must be repaid to the bondholder at maturity. Australian Treasury bonds are issued with face values of $1,000. In some markets, such as the United States, when bond prices are quoted in the financial press, prices are expressed as a percentage of the bond's face value (e.g., $98.50 = $985).
Maturity and repayment of principal	The maturity date refers to the date on which the bond issuer must repay the principal or face value to the bondholder.
Coupon rate	The coupon rate on a bond indicates the percentage of the face value of the bond that will be paid out annually in the form of interest.
Current yield	The current yield on a bond is the rate of return you will receive if you buy the bond at its current price and hold it until maturity. It is the discount rate that equates the present value of the future cash flows from the bond with its current price.
Call provision	Some corporate bonds have a call provision, which provides the issuer of the bond with the right to redeem or retire a bond before it matures.
Conversion feature	In addition, some corporate bonds have a conversion feature that allows bondholders to

	convert their bonds into a set number of ordinary shares.

(Extracted from Titman et al., 2016)

4.7 Short- and long-term loans

Financial institutions will offer loans to their clients. Some of the loans will be offered for short periods, and others will be offered for longer periods. The period to repay the loan is the main difference between short- and long-term loans, but they have many similarities as shown in Figure 6. For one, whether a business owner needs a long- or short-term loan, they must provide the collateral needed by the bank.

Figure 6. Common aspects of short- and long-term loans

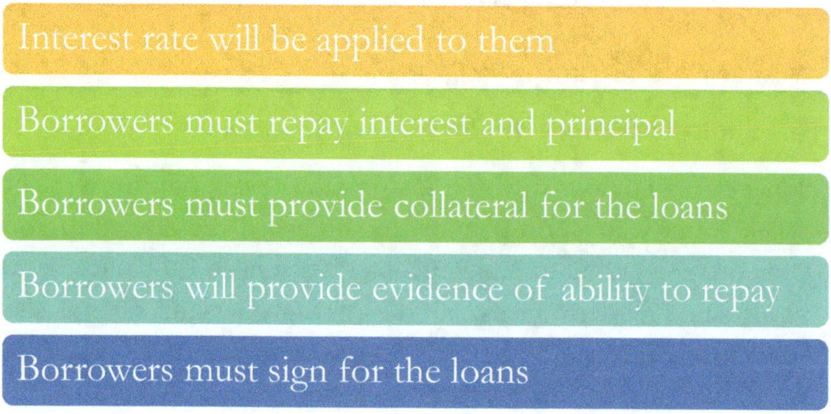

Interest rate will be applied to them

Borrowers must repay interest and principal

Borrowers must provide collateral for the loans

Borrowers will provide evidence of ability to repay

Borrowers must sign for the loans

Some financial institutions may request audited financial statements for short- and long-term loans. Those financial institutions need to know a business's past financial performance before offering them loans. For other financial institutions, audited financial statements of businesses will only be needed for long-term loans.

4.8 Time period to repay

The time period for short-term loans can range from 1 to 24 months. At some financial institutions, short-term loans may even continue to 36 months. Long-term loans will be any loans that go beyond the duration of short-term loans. Therefore, long-term loans usually involve repayment periods longer than 24 months.

4.9 Reasons businesses seek short-term loans

There are several reasons why individuals and business owners will seek short-term loans as shown in Figure 7.

Figure 7. Possible reasons businesses seek short-term loans

Do not want to tie up the funds for longer periods

Cost of investment is small

Business owner is risk neutral

Business is highly leveraged

Uncertainty of the economy

Funds needed for emergency

4.9.1 Do not want to tie up the funds for longer periods

Business owners may choose short-term loans because they do not want to tie up the business's funds for longer periods since that will affect their future plans. Many times, with long-term loans, some collateral will have to be offered for a longer period. The security deposit for long-term loans may be greater than that for short-term loans. Long-term loans will require businesses to allocate parts of their income for longer periods until the loan is fully paid.

4.9.2 Size of investment is small

If the cost of investment is small, then there is no need to seek a long-term loan. For example, if the business owners only need $40,000, then they may seek such a loan for a few months. If the same business needed $4,000,000, then they may seek to acquire the funds for a longer period to give them more time to pay back the loan.

4.9.3 Business owners are risk neutral

Sometimes, business owners will seek investments that have little risk. They may look for investments where they are almost certain of the outcome.

4.9.4 Business is highly leveraged

When businesses are highly leveraged, they may not be entitled to long-term loans. Financial institutions may lend them money but only for a short period because those financial institutions do not want to take too much risk. Long-term loans will demand a longer period of making regular payments.

4.9.5 Uncertainty of the economy

When the economy is going through difficulties, business owners may not want to be involved in major investments, so they will restrict their borrowing to shorter terms. With short-term borrowing during difficult economic situations, the borrower may still find ways to repay the loan in the event the economy suffers further challenges.

4.9.6 Funds needed for emergency

Short-term borrowing may be done in cases of emergency. This will include money to acquire inventory or borrowing money to settle debts with suppliers that are due within short periods. Once those emergencies are over, then there is no need for further loans.

4.10 Possible reasons for long-term loans

Business owners will seek long term loans for different reasons as shown in Figure 8. Some business owners may not be in a rush to settle the amounts they will borrow, so they will seek longer time to repay those loans.

Figure 8. Possible reasons businesses seek long-term loans

> Longer payback periods
>
> Cost of investment is large
>
> Business owner is risk seeker
>
> Business is not highly leveraged
>
> Certainty of the economy
>
> Lower interest rates

4.10.1 Longer payback periods

At times, business owners find that long-term loans are more appropriate for a particular investment. Such loans may put less stress on the business to offset the liability to the financial institution. Instead of repaying the principal over a 24-month period, for example, they have 60 months in which to pay the installments.

4.10.2 Cost of investment is large

When the cost of investment is large, it may be difficult, if not impossible, to repay the loan in a shorter period. For example, constructing a new warehouse may be a costly investment. With such a major investment, the borrower may need 5 to 10 years instead of only 2 years to repay the loan.

4.10.3 Business owners are risk seekers

Some business owners are risk seekers, and they are willing to take on many risks. They are willing to take longer periods to repay the loan because they believe that they will be in business for a long time and will have great rewards in return.

4.10.4 Business is not highly leveraged

When the business does not have any loans or only has small loans, then they are not burdened with high debts. Business owners who are not burdened with high debt will have space to take loans for longer periods since the new loans may be the only long-term debts that they will have on their balance sheets.

4.10.5 Certainty of the economy

If business owners have confidence that the economy will be stable, then they may be comfortable taking loans for longer periods. The business owners are willing to make major investments because they perceive that the economy is stable or will boom, and they expect to constantly earn high revenues for a longer period.

4.10.6 Lower interest rates

Many times, because the cost of investment is high, business owners will seek longer times to repay the money borrowed. With lower interest rates for long-term loans, the borrowers will be repaying smaller installments as compared to repaying loans for shorter durations with higher interest rates. Most financial institutions know that they will earn large sums when they offer loans for longer periods since they can benefit from compound interest.

4.11 Reasons to avoid long-term loans

Every business owner must determine if they want short- or long-term loans. They must assess their businesses and make decisions that are beneficial to those businesses. To that end, these are some reasons why business owners may avoid long-term loans:

- They must pay installments for long periods.
- The accumulated interest may be almost equal to the principal.
- Businesses may not be able to borrow additional amounts until they fully repay the current loan.
- Too many assets may be tied up until the full long-term loan is repaid.
- Too many documents may have to be presented to the financial institution.
- The owners and directors may not want to take long-term risks.

- The economy may be volatile and may change suddenly.

- The country is likely to experience general and regional elections within a few years, and it is possible that the political parties that govern the country will change.

5. Equity financing

Another way business owners may seek financing is through equity financing. However, when they engage in equity financing, they allow other persons and organizations to be part owners of the business. Therefore, the current owners relinquish part of their ownership in exchange for cash investments.

5.1 Repayment period

Debt financing has a date by which the borrower must repay the lender. However, with equity financing, there is no repayment timeline. There is no maturity date to the investment since those who have invested in the equity of the business are now partners in the business.

Business owners may seek equity financing because they do not have to repay those who invest in the business. Those who acquire shares are no longer expecting to be repaid within a specific time since their investment in the business is a long-term investment, unless they want to sell their ownership in the business.

5.2 Shares

Investors who are interested in having ownership in the business can acquire mainly two types of shares: ordinary or preference shares. In some countries, shares are referred to as stocks, and those stocks are traded on a stock market.

According to Titman et al. (2016), "Preference shareholders receive their dividends before any dividends are distributed to the ordinary shareholders, who receive their dividends from whatever is left over."

"Ordinary share: also known as a common share or common stock. An equity instrument that is subordinate to all other classes of equity instruments (IAS 33: 5)."

5.3 Shareholder rights

Shareholders have rights. Their rights are often specified in writing, and they can exercise their rights whenever the need arises.

"The rights that shareholders acquire with their shares are determined by the Company Acts or ordinances of the jurisdiction in which it was incorporated and by the company's articles of association. Although the details vary between countries, ownership of a share broadly provides the right to" (Tricker, 2015):

- Have your name, address, and shareholding entered onto the shareholder members' register
- Receive notice of all shareholder meetings within a specific time
- Receive the formal company accounts, directors' and auditors' reports, and other statutory notices
- Attend shareholders' meeting
- Vote, either in person or by proxy, at all shareholder meetings
- View the company's statutory records, including the register of members; the register of loans charged against the company's assets; the register of directors, officers, and company secretary; and the register of their shared interests
- Receive dividends that have been duly declared for that class of shares.

5.4 Dividends

In return for investing in the company, investors will often receive dividends. The dividends can be paid during the year as interim dividends. Many businesses will assess the financial performance of the business and determine if the business is profitable; then, the managers and directors will propose interim dividends to shareholders. As the managers and directors assess the final financial performance of the business, once the business is profitable, then they may offer a final dividend to shareholders.

Many shareholders maintain their shares with businesses that offers dividends. Therefore, managers and directors must manage the business continually to make profits since dividends are paid after the expenses are accounted for.

Shareholders can expect dividends continuously once they have shares in the business; on the other hand, debt financers will receive interest only for a specific duration. Once the bonds mature, then bondholders are not entitled to interest. However, shareholders may enjoy dividends for many years.

The interest on bonds is fixed, and the bondholders know how much they will receive at specific periods. However, equity holders do not know how much in dividends they will receive. Shareholders can receive more returns than bondholders once the business is profitable, but dividends are never guaranteed to shareholders.

5.5 Initial public offering

Some private business owners have invested all of their money into the business. However, if the owners choose to seek financing, they may consider going public to raise funds. Through this process, they will issue shares to the public in return for the money the public will pay to acquire those shares. In issuing shares to the public, the business has engaged in an initial public offering (IPO). During an IPO, part of the ownership is transferred from the first owners to those who purchased shares of the business.

When a business wants to go public, it must present some information to the public to convince them to invest in the business. This information about the business is commonly referred to as a prospectus. The prospectus is a formal legal document that provides information about the investment offering.

5.6 Selling of rights

Equity holders have the right to sell their stakes in the business. Once they sell their stakes, then they no longer have the same rights with respect to decision making in the business.

6. Leveraging

In some countries, Gearing is the term that is more used. However, there are other countries where Leveraging is also used. These two terms may be interchangeably used according to the country, but they both refer to the same thing.

All business owners need to evaluate their debt against their assets. Many times, business owners will borrow money to manage the business. However, as they borrow money, they increase their debts, and if they are unable to manage the business properly, they will not have enough funds to pay those persons and companies that have lent them money.

Business owners who know that their business will be involved in borrowing must design a policy to guide them and the managers of the business by setting a ceiling for the debt-to-equity ratio. This becomes important because the managers may become overly ambitious and want to borrow large sums of money. Table 4 shows how this ratio is calculated.

Financial leverage/gearing is the use of debt finance to increase the return on equity by using borrowed funds in such a way that the return generated is greater than the cost of servicing the debt. If the return on borrowed funds is less than the cost of servicing the debt, the effect of gearing is to reduce the return on equity. (BPP Learning Media, 2010, p. 260).

Borrowing money is not always a problem, but paying back the full sum on time is where many issues arise. Even large businesses borrow money. However, managing the funds received and the payments to the lender(s) is critical for the borrowers.

Borrowing is said to create financial leverage or gearing. Financial leverage does not affect the risk or the expected return on the firm's assets, but it does push up the risk of the common stock and lead the stockholders to demand a corresponding higher return. (Bradley & Myers, 1991, p. 190)

Table 4. Debt ratio

Types of gearing/leverage	Formula
Debt ratio	Total liabilities/Total assets

(Extracted from Titman et al., 2016)

The calculations for debt ratios will be slightly different for some businesses because they use a slightly different formula. However, the intention of gearing ratios is to compute the business's percentage of indebtedness. When the gearing ratios keep increasing, it is a sign of concern for the owners. Many businesses aim for debt-to-equity ratios between 25% and 40%. However, if that percentage increases, they will have to take quick measures to manage such high indebtedness.

Several ways for business owners to reduce their debt ratios and leverage include increasing profits, repaying some of their debts, and converting debts into equity.

7. Borrowing costs

Business owners and managers must manage their borrowing costs. High borrowing costs can erode the profits of the business.

Most times, shareholders want constant and increasing dividends. However, financing costs must be deducted from the business revenues before dividends are paid.

7.1 Accounting standards for borrowing costs

There are specific International Accounting Standards (IAS) that govern borrowing costs. All businesses who are required to prepare their financial statements to meet the expectations of stakeholders and regulatory authorities must follow the guidelines established in IAS 23. Below is brief information on borrowing costs according to IAS 23.

7.1.1 Recognition

Borrowing costs that are directly attributable to the acquisition, construction, or production of a qualifying asset form part of the cost of that asset and, therefore, should be capitalized. Other borrowing costs are recognized as an expense (Deloitte, 2017).

7.2 Finance costs

In the statement of comprehensive income and expenditure, employees of the finance department will process all costs relating to the borrowing of funds. The terms *borrowing costs* and *finance costs* are interchangeable and used when recording the cost associated with borrowing funds.

The finance cost is an expense to the business and must be accounted for in the correct months and years. Borrowing costs relating to bonds will also be included in the finance cost line in the statement of comprehensive income and expenditure.

Since some financial instruments will have different periods when interest must be paid to the investors, the employees in the finance department must account for the finance costs within different months and quarters.

7.3 Withholding tax on interest paid to investors

The business may establish an arrangement with the investors where withholding tax (WHT) will be deducted before interest is paid to them. In that situation, the investor will receive their net amount, but it is important that the investor be provided with details of the gross amount and the WHT that was deducted so that the investor can file accurate annual taxation returns.

In some businesses, the investors will be paid the full amount of interest applicable to the financial instrument. In this case, the investors will be responsible for calculating their specific WHT and remitting the correct payment to the revenue authority.

In the statement of comprehensive income and expenditure, the finance employees must account for the gross borrowing costs. When posting the entries, they are free to state what portion is the net amount and what portion represents WHT.

8. Managing repayment of borrowed funds

Business owners are delighted when they successfully acquire financing. They know that they have the funds to do the things they want to do to grow the business. However, business owners may become distracted or carried away and misuse the funds. Business owners must remember that when they borrow funds, they have to repay those funds since there can be many negative consequences to them and their businesses if they fail to do so.

8.1 Increased revenues

When business owners borrowed money, they generally need increase their revenues to pay back the debt and grow the business. Those businesses that sell products will expect to benefit from an increase in sales. They will need to increase their marketing in order to attract more customers, who would then be expected to increase revenues.

Most business owners will expect to have additional customers. New customers will generate additional revenues.

8.2 Manage costs constantly

Even if a business is generating strong revenue, it is expected to manage costs. When costs are not managed properly and constantly, then they can escalate, and the money borrowed will not fulfill the intended purpose.

When business owners seek financing, it may be to increase the efficiency of their operation. For example, the business owners may plan to replace outdated equipment and machinery. With those replacements, they can then reduce their operational costs.

Replacing some machinery and equipment can result in an increase in production. When costs are reduced, businesses can be more competitive, and customers can expect to enjoy lower selling prices.

8.3 Generating steady and increasing profits

Profit is derived by deducting costs from revenues. If business owners want more profits, then they must increase their revenue with the same costs or keep revenue constant but reduce costs. The business owners, along with the managers, must measure the growth of the business. At least two ways of measuring growth in a business are through an increase in profitability and revenues. Additional measurements are listed in Table 5.

Table 5. Some ways of measuring growth for an organization

Area of growth	Comment
Revenue	In the long term, growth in revenue is only really valuable to investors if it means growth in profits.
Profitability	Growing profitability is more useful if it is related to the level of investment.
Return on investment	A growing return on investment suggests that capital is being used more productively.
Market share	Growth in market shares is generally regarded as a good thing as it can generate economies of scale.
Number of employees	Shareholders are interested in productivity and profit per employee. An increasing head count is a measure of success if people are needed to deliver a service, but people need to be employed productively.

Number of products	Growth in the number of products is only useful if the products are profitable.
Cash flow	This is one of the most important measures of growth as it ultimately determines how much a business has to invest.

(Extracted from BPP Learning Media, 2010)

Business owners generally spend much of their time increasing their profits. They will try to improve the efficiency of the business or generate more revenues.

8.4 Timely repayment of borrowed funds

When businesses borrow funds, the owners must remember to repay those funds in a timely manner. Business owners must ensure that they are generating enough profits and cash flow to repay the loans. Lenders will continue to support borrowers who have honored their obligations. If business owners need financing for the future, their previous repayment history will impact their ability to borrow once again.

8.5 Use funds for intended purposes

One of the great challenges many borrowers are faced with is the temptation to use the borrowed funds for another purpose. There are many emergencies that often appear after funds are received. However, if the business owners are disciplined and use the funds for their intended purposes, then they are likely to achieve their intended goals.

Section 2: Investments and projects

A thorough understanding of project costs is important for business owners and managers. The costs for the project must be carefully assessed. Once the costs are approved for the budget, then the managers must monitor those costs. Regular reports must be provided for the comparison between actual and budgeted costs.

Moreover, time must be allocated to projects. This time is critical because it can determine how long the money must be borrowed. Many times, the payback period for the money borrowed must exceed the time when the project will be completed.

Before embarking on capital investments, managers must present enough information to prove that the investment is viable. Before executing any capital investment, managers must evaluate the business using several capital budgeting techniques.

9. Project costs

A project is a temporary endeavour undertaken to create a unique product, service or result. The temporary nature of projects indicates a definite beginning and end. The end is reached when the project's objectives have been achieved or when the project is terminated because its objectives will not or cannot be met, or when the need for the project no longer exists. (PMI, 2008)

Whenever business owners are considering projects, they must consider the costs. These costs must be known upfront before approval is granted. Many persons are often amazed when they add together all the costs and see how much it will cost them to complete the project.

Project cost management includes the processes involved in estimating, budgeting, and controlling cost so that the project can be completed within the approved budget. Project cost management is primarily concerned with the cost of the resources needed to complete project activities. (PMI, 2008)

9.1 Estimating costs

First, managers must gather all the relevant costs for the project. They may be required to engage in research, especially if they are about to embark on something that is totally new to them. For example, if the owners need a warehouse, and it is the first time that the business will have its own warehouse, information will be needed from internal and external sources to determine all of the involved costs.

Each activity for the project must be assigned a cost. It may be impossible to know the precise cost at the time when the estimate is being prepared, but reasonable costs must be included in the estimates.

When preparing estimated costs, managers must consider price inflation since it is likely that the costs will increase during the implementation phase of the project. Managers may also include a contingency cost in their estimates. The contingency cost will be used as a buffer in the event there are changes in the actual cost and/or for costs that could not be foreseen at the time when the estimate was prepared.

Wherever possible, managers must provide details for the project costs. This will include units and cost per unit. Therefore, each activity will be multiplied by the unit cost to provide the total cost per activity. For example, 20 labor hours at $50 per hour will result in an estimated cost of $1,000.

For some projects, managers and owners may need to recruit the service of a consultant. The consultant will provide technical services, so the consultant's cost must be included in the estimate.

9.2 Determining budget

The second part of the project cost is to prepare the budget for the project. The budget will include the aggregate of the individual estimated costs. The budget must be prepared in a professional manner for the business owners to evaluate the project.

When reviewing the budget, managers must have the estimated costs available to provide details if the need arises. Many times, when business owners see large costs, they want to know how those costs were derived. When owners can see and hear about these details, then they can make a more informed decision to proceed with the project as-is or to ask for the project to be modified.

After business owners review the project costs, they may agree to execute the project in phases. For example, Phase 1 will be executed in Year 1 and Phase 2 in the following year. When the initial funds for the project are invested, then the owners must carefully manage how much they can set aside for the execution of the project.

There are some projects that cannot be completed in phases. Thus, if there are not enough total funds in the budget, then the business owners will have to seek financing if they want to execute these projects.

9.3 Controlling costs

Some activities and projects are easier to plan than others. Once approval is given for the project to be executed, then the costs for the project must be monitored. If costs are not monitored, then the project's actual costs can exceed the amount budgeted.

Many projects suffer from cost overruns. The managers fail to monitor the costs throughout the project cycle, and/or some of the costs increase significantly during the time of execution.

If there are delays in executing the project after the project budget is determined, then the project budget must be revised before the project progresses. For example, if the prices for many of the activities are affected by inflation, then any delay by a few months can result in the costs for those activities increasing significantly.

In controlling the project costs, managers must regularly collect costs and analyze them against the budget. There will often be a variance.

Variances are the difference between actual results and expected results. When actual results are better than we expect, we have a favourable variance, and when actual results are worse than we expect, we have an adverse variance. (BPP Business Education, 1997)

If the project costs keep increasing, then the owners and managers must take action. They can continue with the project, stop the project, amend the scope of the project, or fast-track the project. However, if the project costs are not presented regularly, then the owners will not be aware that the project is experiencing cost overruns and thus will be unable to take corrective actions.

9.4 Rate of Exchange

If products and services have to be sourced from overseas, then the rate of exchange (ROE) will have an impact on the project cost. The rate of exchange can suddenly fluctuate, especially if there are external factors that affect countries.

9.5 Submit costs in local currency

Even if most of the activities and products needed will be procured from a foreign country, the presentation of the budget must include the costs in the business's local currency. Additionally, the managers will need to constantly monitor the rates of exchange when presenting the local currency costs.

10. Project time

Projects will incur time. The time for many projects varies, but time must be taken into consideration.

10.1 Project activities and durations

With some projects, the duration may be a few days or a few months. There are other projects where the duration will span many years.

The activities and duration of the project must be provided, and the duration can be presented using a Gantt chart.

A Gantt chart is a kind of horizontal bar chart where the length of the bar represents the duration of the activity. When a Gantt chart is used to help in the control of a project, two bars are used to represent each activity—one the planned duration and the other the actual duration. (BPP Professional Education, 2003)

10.2 Estimating activity durations

When the project is divided into activities, then each activity must be given a timeline. Some projects are likely to be completed within the planned time; however, there are other projects where the duration can be very lengthy and unpredictable. For example, the construction of a building, warehouse, or bridge may span many months or years.

The longer the project takes to complete, the greater is the possibility that the costs will increase. Therefore, the owners along with the managers may agree to compress the project. Table 6 lists two common compression strategies.

Table 6. Scheduling compression of project

Term	Explanation
Crashing	A schedule compression technique in which cost and schedule trade-offs are analyzed and determined to obtain the greatest amount of compression for the least incremental cost. Examples of crashing include approving overtime, bringing in additional resources, or paying to expedite delivery to activities on the critical path.
Fast tracking	A schedule compression technique in which phases or activities normally performed in the sequence are performed in parallel. An example is constructing the foundation for a building before completing all the architectural drawings.

(Extracted from PMI, 2008)

If the project goes beyond the projected time, then the expected benefits or revenues will be delayed or reduced. Some projects are executed to increase the revenue of the business such as the construction of a new store. If the construction of the new store is delayed, then every day that there is a delay, sales will be lost. Potential customers may choose to shop at other stores and become loyal to those simply because a business was not able to open its doors on time.

If the project will result in cost reductions because some aspects of the business become more efficient, then any delay in the start time will result in the business's continuing to experience higher costs. When money is borrowed to complete projects, then the owners and the managers must seek to complete the project on or before the projected time.

11. Capital investments

Business owners often borrow money for capital investments. Usually, funds borrowed for long-term investments will be repaid over longer durations. Short-term borrowing will often be used to fill any urgent gaps. Some of those short-term gaps that must be filled include acquiring inventory for an upcoming season, repaying suppliers, or replacing an expensive part. However, when business owners need to make major investments, then they need large amounts of financing that can be repaid over long durations.

As a business becomes successful and profitable, owners will often save funds that they can use to embark on capital investments, often in conjunction with outside financing. Figure 9 shows the main types of capital investments owners make.

Figure 9. Types of capital-investment projects

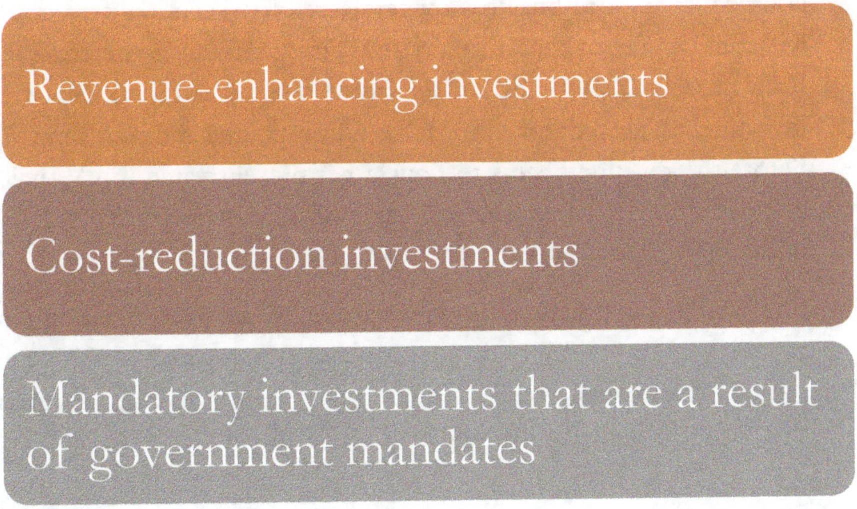

(Extracted from Titman et al., 2016)

11.1 Capital investment approvals

Managers may suggest to the owners the need for capital investments. The owners may verbally agree to those investments but ask the managers to prepare a proposal for review and approval.

If the managers do not have the capability to provide all the information needed for the proposal, then they can seek external assistance. The proposal must cover all possible costs and revenues. The managers will have to provide written information about the proposal. Along with the written information, the managers will verbally discuss the proposal with the owners. The business owners will read the proposal and listen to the managers' presentations. Once the managers provide accurate and compelling reports to the business owners, then the business owners will consider approving the capital investment. Usually, business owners will agree to include capital investments in the annual budget.

11.2 Potential revenues

When business owners engage in capital expenditures, they are considering that the investment will generate significant cash inflows and profits. Before business owners agree to execute a project, they will conduct a cost-benefit analysis. Their intention is to determine the likely revenues and expenses from the investment. Since the investment will take some time to be fully executed and thus some time before the revenue begins to flow, a net present value (NPV) will be computed to determine the real value of money that will be received in the future. (See Table 7.)

The owners must take all possible revenues into consideration when assessing if they will go ahead with capital investments. With some capital investments, there are numerous ancillary sources of revenue that will be obtained from one major investment.

11.3 Greater efficiency

Major investments will likely be approved if they will enable the business to be more efficient in its operation. Perhaps some costs of the business will be reduced, or there will be faster turnaround times for some business processes.

If the owners agree to acquire state-of-the-art machinery, then the production costs for the business will likely decline. Since employment costs such as salaries generally increase each year, business owners may plan to use capital investments in efficient machinery to utilize fewer employees and reduce overtime hours.

If the business has many machines and vehicles that suffer from regular breakdowns, then the business owners may choose to replace those machines and vehicles. Acquiring new vehicles will be an expensive investment, but the benefits are often great and will allow the business to reduce costs and have better efficiency over time.

11.4 Evaluating capital investments

Managers and business owners must evaluate each investment, and there are several techniques for doing so. Each of the capital budgeting techniques used to evaluate investments has its own advantages and disadvantages as shown in Table 7.

Table 7. Basic capital budgeting techniques

Investment criterion	Definition	Decision rule	Advantages	Disadvantages
Net present value (NPV)	Present value of expected cash inflows minus present value of	Accept investments that have positive NPV	Theoretically correct in that it directly measures the increase in value that the project	Somewhat complicated to compute (requires an understanding of the time value of money);

	cash outflows		is expected to produce; measures the increase in shareholder wealth expected from undertaking the project being analyzed	unfamiliar to managers without formal business education
Equivalent annual cost (EAC) or equivalent annual annuity (EAA)	The annual cost equivalent in present value to the initial cost and annual cash flows of an investment	Select the investment alternative that has the lowest annual cost	Provides a tool that can be used to account for differences in the initial cost of purchase, different annual costs of operations and different productive lives	Should only be used where the investments being compared are expected to be used indefinitely (for single-use investments, NPV is appropriate)
Profitability index (PI)	Present value of expected future cash flows divided by	Accept the project when the PI is greater than 1 as	Theoretically correct in that it directly measures the increase	Not as familiar to managers as NPV

	the initial cash investment	the NPV will be positive; reject the project when the PI is less than 1 as this indicates a poor investment and the NPV will be negative	in value that the project is expected to produce; useful when ranking positive-NPV projects where capital is being rationed	
Internal rate of return (IRR)	The discount rate that makes NPV equal to zero	Accept the project if the IRR is greater than the required rate of return or the discount rate used to calculate the NPV of the project; reject the project otherwise	Provides a rate-of-return metric, which many managers prefer	Cannot always be estimated; sometimes provides multiple rates of return for projects with multiple changes in the sign of their cash flows overtime; can provide conflicting indications to NPV for mutually

				exclusive projects
Modified internal rate of return (MIRR)	The discount rate that makes the NPV of the modified cash-flow stream equal to zero	Accept the project if the MIRR is greater than the required rate of return or the discount rate used to calculate the NPV of the project; reject the project otherwise	Always produces a single rate-of-return estimate	The rate of return produced by the MIRR not unique to the project because it is influenced by the discount rate used to discount the negative cash flows
Payback period	Time until the initial cash outlay has been recovered	Accept the project If the project payback is less than the maximum the firm will accept	Easy to understand and calculate; an indication of risk (how long it takes to recover the investment)	Ignores time value of money and cash flows beyond the payback period; no rational way to determine the cut-off value for payback

Discounted payback period	The number of years required to recover the initial investment out of the project's discounted future cash flows	Accept the project if the discounted project payback is less than the maximum the firm will accept	Same as for payable period; also considers the time value of money by discounting the cash flows	Ignores cash flows beyond the payback period; no rational way to determine the cut-off value for payback; also involves a more complicated payback period to compute for as cash inflows must be discounted

(Extracted from BPP Learning Media, 2010)

11.5 Viable investments

Before agreeing on the capital investment, owners want to see that the computation proves that the investment is viable. The investment must produce a profit and net positive cash inflow. Investors want to know that they are earning money, rather than losing money, from their capital investments.

Business owners will not invest their money into projects that are constantly making losses. Moreover, since the money used for many investments will be borrowed funds, the investments must provide positive net cash inflows.

11.6 Net cash inflows

The capital investment must generate new cash inflows. It is through the net cash inflows that business owners will repay any financing that was taken out or replace the funds previously used from the business.

Generating profits is not enough, though. Businesses need to generate net cash inflows so that their wealth will increase. Profits can be distorted by accounting entries, but net cash inflow is money that is available to spend.

11.7 Examples of capital investments

Business owners will have many projects in which they will invest their money. Whatever capital investments they choose, they must evaluate each investment. A business can have several capital investments running at the same time. Some of the capital investments will run for long periods and will be very expensive while other capital investments will not require the same amount of financing and duration.

Capital investments are useful for new and existing operations. These are some examples:

- Acquisition of land and buildings
- New or expanded warehouses
- New fleet of vehicles
- New computers
- Acquisition of an integrated information system
- New stores and branches
- Acquisition of furniture

Section 3: Cash management and financial ratios

Managing cash and bank balances is important in every business. If the business has excess funds, then such funds can be used for further investments or be deposited into bank accounts that generate reasonable interest. When depositing excess money, managers must ensure that they carefully manage the cash inflows and outflows of the business. In the case of emergencies, managers must be able to access the funds from the deposit accounts.

12. Managing cash and bank balances

Cash remains a critical resource to any business. Even non-profit organizations need cash to manage their businesses; for example, schools need cash for their regular activities. Just as an individual needs cash to pay for public transportation or to purchase fuel for a vehicle, so too does a business need cash for daily operations.

12.1 Cash forecasting

Managers must review their cash and bank balances and project the funds they need to manage the business. Based on the cash forecast, they will understand any gaps that are likely to occur.

A source of cash is any activity that brings cash into the firm, such as when the firm sells goods and services or sells an old piece of equipment that it no longer needs. A use of cash is any activity that causes cash to leave the firm, such as the payment of tax, the purchase of a new piece of equipment, and so forth. (Titman et al., 2016, p. 60)

Cash forecasting is important to all businesses. It allows the managers and owners to know their projected inflows, outflows, and balances. If the outflows are greater than the inflows, then additional funds will be needed for specific periods. When inflows are greater than outflows, then the temporary excess funds must be saved or reinvested.

If the owners perceive that there will be a cash shortage, then efforts must be made to forecast increases in sales. Businesses that have products to sell must use those products to generate the additional cash the business needs. Sometimes the decision to increase promotion may be a good response to increase sales. If the current products are not selling fast at the current prices, then adding giveaways may stir customers' interest to buy more products. Moreover, customers will often buy more if they know that discounts will be available to them. Offering discounts and giveaways can boost sales, which will allow for more cash to flow into the business.

If the business has a large value of accounts receivables, then reminders can be sent to those credit customers to settle their balances in a timely manner. Customers that owe the business money can be offered the opportunity to settle their balances at a discounted sum. This approach may be taken to incentivize credit customers to pay their balances before the due date.

If it is perceived that the business will be out of cash for short or long periods, then short-term and long-term borrowing must be considered. The purpose of borrowing would then be to fill the forecasted gaps and invest in any other strategic business opportunities.

12.2 Submission of regular cash and bank balances

Both cash and bank balances must be reviewed regularly. The reviews must be part of the business's internal controls. At many businesses, the person heading the finance department (often the chief financial officer [CFO]) will be presented with the cash and bank balances at least once per week. The cash and bank balances will then be submitted to the chief executive officer (CEO) or managing director (MD).

Regular submission of the cash and bank balances must be evaluated against the cash forecast. In some organizations, one report may be designed to include the cash and bank balances and the cash forecast.

12.3 Bank reconciliations

Bank reconciliations must be done at least monthly. Some have designated employees who are responsible for the preparation of bank reconciliations, and those employees may be engaged in weekly or daily bank reconciliations. This is another important internal control.

The completed bank reconciliation provides evidence of the true bank balances. There are often timing differences with some bank transactions, so the bank reconciliation will identify those transactions.

Some small business owners prefer to keep all their cash on hand; however, they should consider banking their money for several reasons as shown in Figure 10.

Figure 10. Reasons why banking may be necessary for organizations

National security policy

Frequent circulation of conterfiet notes

Points gained for money regularly deposited and large amounts saved

Easy access to pay suppliers via bank payments

Payment of utility and employment costs through the bank

International and regional payments that must be done through the bank

In many businesses, there are procedures that govern the preparation of bank reconciliations. These procedures are unique to those businesses and provide guidance on how bank reconciliations must be prepared and the need to clear outstanding transactions.

12.4 Online banking

Traditionally, many business owners enjoyed customers' visiting their businesses and paying for the products or services they needed in person. Today, however, there is the option for customers to make online payments. With online payments, business owners no longer must wonder about timely payments or counterfeit payments. Online payments allow the funds to be directly deposited to the bank without any employees of the business having to make daily bank deposits on behalf of the business.

Online banking allows businesses to see the funds' movement in their bank accounts. Managers can pay suppliers and utility companies via online banking. Employees' remunerations are also sent online to their respective bank accounts.

Online banking has made bank reconciliations much simpler. Those bank reconciliations have fewer outstanding transactions since many of the transactions are processed directly to the designated recipient account, or the bank reconciliation will identify and take immediate action for any incoming funds.

12.5 Safeguarding cash received

When cash is received, it must be protected since stolen cash is difficult or impossible to retrieve. Also, persons are often easily tempted with cash. Therefore, the managers and business owners must protect the cash they receive.

If cash is kept in the safe, then dual custody will be important to prevent one person from illegally removing the money. The safe must be a fireproof safe, so in the event of fire, the contents are protected.

Any cash and checks received on the business's behalf must be secured and banked at the earliest date. A small portion of cash may be kept for the purpose of petty cash or to act as a float for the cashier's daily transactions.

13. Savings

Although some businesses have limited cash, there are other businesses that have excess cash and few major expenses. Business owners who have made major investments in the past may now be benefiting from their investments. The operations at some businesses are efficient, so they incur fewer costs and more profits.

13.1 Excess cash

When there is excess cash, business owners must decide what to do with it.

Extra cash must be carefully used or saved. Extra cash can be saved in local banks or in foreign banks, where the business owners may earn higher interest rates. Although there may be extra cash now, there may be sudden need for the extra cash, so business owners must ensure that they can quickly access their cash when the need arises.

When saving extra cash, business owners must ensure that they receive reasonable benefits in return. They should verify that the institution where they are saving their money is a safe place. No one wants the misfortune of placing their money into a savings account at a financial institution only for that institution to file for bankruptcy.

13.2 Interest rates on deposits

Before placing extra money into deposit accounts, business owners must evaluate the interest rates they will be receiving for their savings. The interest rate on a deposit is often affected by the amount deposited and the duration of the deposit.

The interest rate will often vary across financial institutions. Therefore, business owners must gather enough information about the various interest rates from the different financial institutions before choosing where to save their money.

If we assume an investment will earn interest only on the original principal, we call this **simple interest.** The process of accumulating interest on an investment over multiple periods is called **compounding**, [and] when interest is earned on both the initial principal and the reinvested interest during prior periods, the result is called compound **interest.** (Titman et al., 2016, p. 133)

13.3 Duration of savings

In some cases, business owners can earn higher interest rates if they commit to leaving their funds saved or invested for longer durations. For example, one financial institution may offer 0.50% for money saved for 6 months. However, if the same amount is saved for 1 year, then the interest rate may be 0.75%. Most financial institutions are delighted when they have the money to use for longer durations. In return, those financial institutions will offer higher interest rates to those individuals and businesses that will save with them for longer durations. In some countries, the interest rate is fixed for savings held for a one year duration. However, in other countries, financial institutions offer different interest rates for savings held within a one year duration.

Table 8. Varying interest for the same savings

Duration	Amount ($)	Rate (%)
1–180 days	100,000	0.25
181–360 days	100,000	0.50
Over 360 days	100,000	0.75

13.4 Accounting for interest received from savings

When interest is received, it must be accounted for in the business's statement of comprehensive income and statement of financial position. The general ledger entries will credit the income account and debit the bank account. Figure 11 shows this process.

Figure 11. Impact on financial statements of interest received from savings

14. Financial ratios

Managers have many options for analyzing the business. When managers work many years with the same business, there are some things that they can quickly determine even without having access to much data.

Although experience in the business is helpful, employees may not always diagnose many of the successes and shortfalls of the business. Each manager will assess those areas with which they are comfortable. However, financial ratios enable all managers and owners to analyze many segments of the business in a straightforward, objective manner.

Many persons can analyze the business using financial ratios. Those persons neither have to know the details of the business nor have previous working experience in the business. The financial ratios can be used by external stakeholders to determine shortfalls or successes of the business. Financial ratios also can be used for businesses that operate in different countries, and they will still reveal accurate information across borders.

14.1 Categories of financial ratios

There are many financial ratios that can be used to assess different segments of the business different aspects of the financial performance of the business. The same ratios can be used every year. It is important to assess the financial performance of the business by comparing one year with the next in order to see progress or decline. When financial ratios are calculated only for one financial year, it becomes impossible to properly assess the business since one-year financial performance will not show any basis for comparison. Table 9 lists several key financial ratios that are commonly used to assess businesses.

Table 9. Financial ratios examples

Category of financial ratio (Summary)	Category of financial ratio (detail)	Category of financial ratio (formula)
Liquidity	Current ratio	Current assets/Current liabilities
	Quick ratio	Current assets (inventory)/Current liabilities
	Average collection period	Accounts receivable/Annual credit sales
	Accounts receivable turnover	Annual credit sales/Accounts receivable
	Inventory turnover	Cost of goods sold/Inventory
Capital structure ratios	Debt ratio	Total liabilities/Total assets
	Interest coverage ratio	Operating profit or EBIT/Interest expense
Asset management efficiency ratios	Total assets turnover	Sales/Total assets
	Fixed asset turnover	Sales/Net property, plant and equipment

Profitability ratio	Gross profit ratio	Gross profit/Sales
	Operating profit margin	Operating profit or EBIT/Sales
	Net profit margin	Net profit/Sales
	Return on assets	Operating profit or EBIT/Total assets
	Return on equity	Net profit/Ordinary equity
Market value ratio	Price-earnings ratio	Market price per share/Earnings per share
	Market-to-book ratio	Market price per share/Book value per share

(Extracted from Titman et al., 2016)

The ratios present key information to the managers and owners. For example, if they want to know if the business is highly indebted, they can use the debt ratio. If they want to know if the business is liquid, then they can use the current and quick ratios.

When managers present monthly accounts and financial reports to the owners, they often use variance analysis. The variance analysis will be explained in the commentaries of their reports. The managers can evaluate the business with different ratios, and the results from those ratios can also be presented to the business owners.

There are no restrictions on how many ratios can be used to analyze a business. Often, managers will use a variety of ratios that cover different aspects of the financial performance of the business to give the owners a fuller and more nuanced view of the business's progress.

14.2 Ratios have limitations

Financial ratios are useful for evaluating the business, but they do have limitations as depicted in Figure 12.

Figure 12. Limitations of ratio analysis

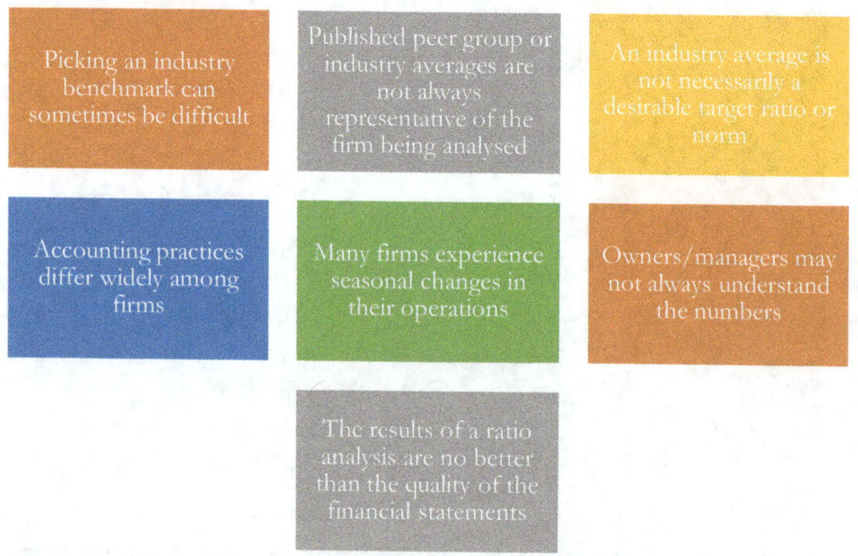

(Extracted from Titman et al., 2016)

References

BPP Business Education. (1997). *Cat paper B2 – level B: Cost accounting systems: Interactive text*. BPP Business Education Ltd.

BPP Learning Media. (2010). *ACCA paper P5 advanced performance management: Practice and revision kit*. BPP Learning Media Ltd.

BPP Professional Education. (2003). *ACCA paper 3.4 business information management: Study text*. BPP Publishing Ltd.

Bradley, R. A., & Myers, S. C. (1991). *Principles of corporate finance* (4th ed.). McGraw-Hill.

Deloitte. (2009). *IAS 33--earnings per share*. Deloitte. https://www.iasplus.com/en/standards/ias/ias33

Deloitte. (2017). *IAS 23--borrowing costs*. Deloitte. https://www.iasplus.com/en/standards/ias/ias23

Loughram, M. (2011). *Financial accounting for dummies*. John Wiley & Sons.

Project Management Institute (PMI). (2008). *A guide to project management book of knowledge (PMBOK)* (4th ed.). Project Management Institute.

Titman, S., Martin, T., Keown, A. J., & Martin, J. D. (2016). *Financial management: Principles and applications* (7th ed.). Pearson Australia.

Tricker, B. (2015). *Corporate governance: Principles, policies and practices* (3rd ed.). Oxford University Press.

About the author

After working with businesses that struggled to meet their financial needs, chartered accountant Geary Reid has firsthand experience with those financial challenges. He worked along with managers and business owners to move their businesses away from being highly indebted to having adequate finances to manage their operations. After working for businesses that found it difficult to pay employees their salaries and wages on time, Geary Reid believes that business owners and managers must work towards increasing the profits and cash flows of their businesses.

Geary Reid appreciates many of the struggles business owners have in understanding the technical issues concerning borrowing and investments, so he decided to provide them with a simple primer on these topics. He provides numerous examples to enhance their understanding of business financing, because of his studies and regular dealings concerning financing and investments. Often, business owners fail to obtain financing for their businesses because they are not aware of some of the requirements needed when seeking financing, so Geary has made sure that this book covers such important topics in depth.

Geary also provides business owners with information to determine if short- or long-term loans are right for them and explains each option's requirements. Geary Reid wants to encourage managers and business owners to use the funds borrowed for their intended purposes. Over his years of experience, Geary Reid has implemented many of these ratios and formats that easily identify and assess a business's financial health. In the commentaries he prepared on the business's financial performance, he explains the variance and provides suggestions for improvements.